Captain Howard's Story Time Books

Tom Turtle
Win - Place - Show

By Captain Howard C. Williams

Howard is the holder of an O.U.P.V. Boat Captain License.

AuthorHouse™
1663 Liberty Drive
Bloomington, IN 47403
www.authorhouse.com
Phone: 1 (800) 839-8640

This book is printed on acid-free paper.

ISBN: 978-1-7283-2669-6 (sc)
ISBN: 978-1-7283-2670-2 (hc)
ISBN: 978-1-7283-2668-9 (e)

Library of Congress Control Number: 2019913867

Print information available on the last page.

Published by AuthorHouse 10/04/2019

authorHOUSE®

Dedication

This book was originally written for my youngest daughter Leah over two decades ago...I would like to dedicate it to her, her sisters Lynai and Lori, and their children totaling eight grandchildren and one great-grandchild.

Grandchildren: Imara, Alexis, Ishmael, Carlyn, Sierra, Andre, Eddie and Amir.

Great-grandchild: London

Acknowledgements

My special thanks to Debbie Jones, for without her unwavering commitment to help see this book through, it would not have been published.

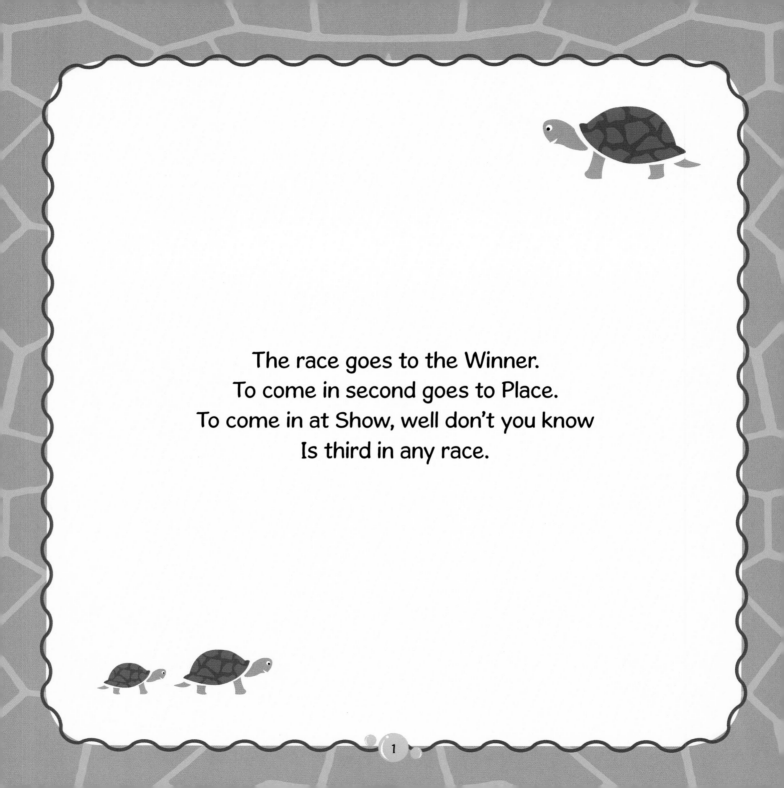

The race goes to the Winner.
To come in second goes to Place.
To come in at Show, well don't you know
Is third in any race.

Well Tom had never won a race
But he did come in at Show
Not Win, not Place
But there was a race
How to win that Tom did know.
The reason for his tardiness
What on Earth could it ever be.
Well no one knew like Tommy knew
And as you read on you'll see.

When Tom was born a hatchling
And peeked from his turtle shell
He looked up to the sky above
And vowed, he'd learn his lessons well.
Well Tom lived up to that
In his slow Tom Turtle way.
He's the smartest turtle ever born
He's the smartest till today.

When it came time to go to turtle school
Now, there Tom he'd be first.

He'd wake up early, wash his face,
Put on his turtle pants and shirt.

He'd slowly brush his turtle teeth
First turtle tooth to the turtle last.

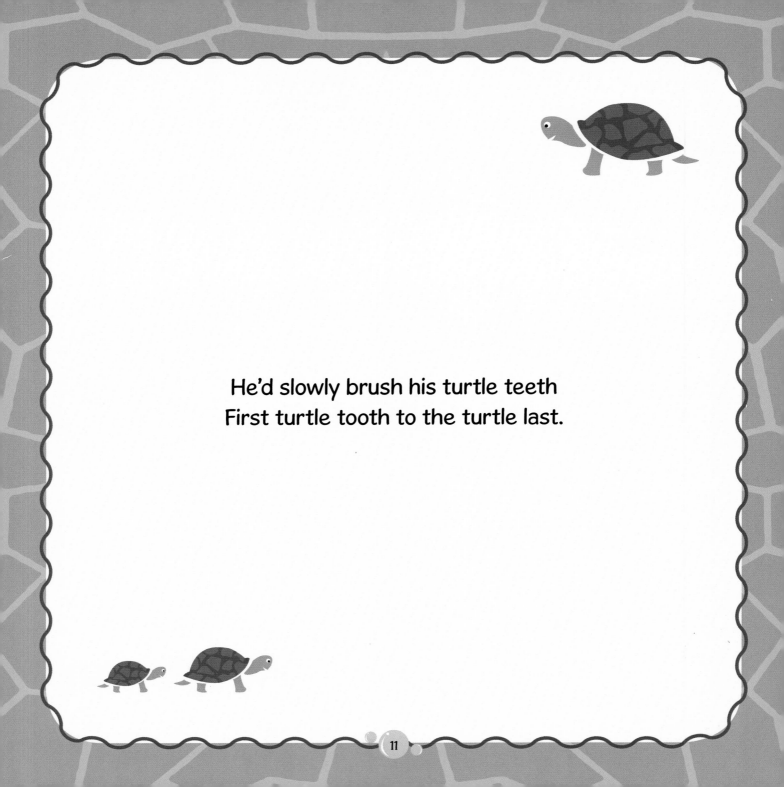

And off to turtle school he'd go
Turtle slow, not turtle fast.
Now Tommy was a slowpoke
Who always seemed to win.
He'd go so slow, to and fro
You'd rarely notice him.

He studied very carefully
No matter what the task.
He paid attention to the details
So he never came in last.

Yes Tom, he was a scholar
He loved his turtle school.
He always knew when he grew up
He'd be no turtle fool.
His Mom was very proud of him
His father, he was too.

He could name them every animal
They had in turtle zoo.

Now who would know, that going slow
could be better and not worse.
Well those who knew, and followed through
Like Tommy came in first.
To take his time
Young Tommy knew
That he would gain more knowledge,
And that's exactly what it did for him
Till he left Turtle College.

There's a lesson to be learned
In going slow sometimes, not fast.
Take it from Tommy Turtle
Tip Top of his Turtle class.

About the Author

Born Howard Courtney Williams, son of Jamaican immigrants, Captain Howard grew up in Harlem, New York. His love of nature was nurtured through his decade-long association with the Boy Scouts of America. As his suburban and rural outdoor activities increased his observance and understanding of nature became as important to him as surviving life as a city dweller. When Captain Howard could not leave for the suburbs he regularly fished the local waters throughout all five boroughs of New York City, including the rivers surrounding Manhattan Island. He spent long hours in the large parks, such as Edgecombe Park in Washington Heights and Van Cortlandt Park in the Bronx. He walked the trails and observed the abundant wildlife that most city dwellers never knew existed in their own backyards.

Captain Howard was a New York City union plasterer and drywall finisher for over thirty years before becoming a commodity options pit trader at the Chicago Mercantile Exchange. He was also an independent tractor-trailer driver for many years. Later, he became an independent charter fishing boat captain before retiring in south Florida. Captain Howard's diverse work background and hobbies add flavor to his works, which include more than one hundred poems and short stories, seven children's books, and two novels. He now spends most of his time on the water fishing and relaxing, and writing stories to entertain his grandchildren, great grandchildren, and any other little souls who happen upon his books.

Printed in the United States
By Bookmasters